Optimizing Database Queries

SQL Indexing Techniques

Table of Contents

Chapter 1. Introduction

In this Special Report, we delve into the intricate world of database optimization, specifically focusing on 'SQL Indexing Techniques'. Databases are the keystone of any software system, holding invaluable information that drives business decisions. As such, performance bottlenecks related to querying databases can have a major impact. Therefore, proficient indexing techniques are crucial, not only technically, but also at the strategic level of any project. This practical guide brings you the most effective techniques in query optimization using SQL indexing. We do not need to be a team of tech experts to appreciate its benefits. The report is designed in an easy-to-understand language, highlighting ways to ensure quick data retrieval and increased system performance. A resilient and responsive database system is a realistic goal, and with this Special Report, we are one step closer to achieving it. Don't miss this opportunity to level-up your data management skills and strategies. Embark on this enlightening journey with us. Now, more than ever, efficient use of data is pivotal—and this report equips you with the arsenal to meet these demands head on.

Chapter 2. Understanding Databases and SQL

Chances are, if you're interested in optimizing your data management strategies, you've heard about databases and SQL—or Structured Query Language. These are key pillars for handling structured data, particularly in large scale. So, let's start from basics, then dive deeper into how databases work and how SQL plays a role in data manipulation.

2.1. The Concept of Databases

A database, in its simplest form, is a structured set of data. So, if data is the lifeblood of a business, a database is the heart storing and pumping it, ensuring it gets where it needs to when it needs to be there.

Databases are often categorized into several types based on their data models. For instance, we have relational databases such as MySQL, Oracle, and MS SQL Server that design databases in tabular form. NoSQL databases such as MongoDB, CouchDB, and Cassandra, which are document-based, and graph databases such as Neo4J, which prioritize the relationships between data points.

However, for the purpose of our focus on SQL Indexing Techniques, we'll be majoring on relational databases, which employ SQL for database queries.

2.2. Understanding SQL

SQL, the Structured Query Language, is the standard language used to communicate or interact with a database, particularly relational databases. SQL queries are used to perform various tasks like creating a database, creating tables, inserting data into a table, updating data, deleting data, and retrieving data, among others.

Imagine SQL as the direct communication line between you and your database – it interprets your requests, interacts with the database to fulfill these requests, and presents the results back to you in an understandable format.

2.3. The Fundamentals of Database Optimization

Now that we have an understanding of databases and SQL, how do we ensure the delivery of information is fast, efficient, and accurate to avoid performance bottlenecks?

This calls for database optimization, which involves the modification of a database system to enhance its overall performance and operation. Database optimization addresses factors such as data integrity, performance efficiency, data access speed, resource utilization, and more.

The goal is to reduce latency and improve throughput so that the database system can respond quickly to any given query. From server hardware considerations to software configurations, indexing strategies, and schema design, various aspects come into play when optimizing databases.

2.4. SQL Indexing: A Prime Optimization Strategy

Indexing is an effective technique to speed up the data retrieval process in a database. An SQL index is somewhat similar to an index in a book: instead of scanning the entire book to find a topic, you refer to the index, which guides you directly to the page you need.

In SQL, create an index on a column in your database table, and when you query data from the table, SQL Server would first check the index, leading to faster data retrieval rather than scanning the entire table. This significantly reduces the time and resources required to retrieve data, leading to performance gains in your database operations.

Over the course of this report, we'll delve further into the intricacies of SQL indexing, including understanding how indexes work, when to use them, the various types of indexes, and some best practices for indexing.

Remember, a proficient database system isn't just about the storage, manipulation, and retrieval of data; it's about doing all these tasks efficiently and effectively. With a clear understanding of databases and SQL, you're now better equipped to appreciate the benefits derived from SQL Indexing and other optimization techniques.

Our next chapter will focus on 'The Nitty-gritty of Database Indexing', where we'll break down the concept of indexing and examine how it works to enhance database performance. From the types of indexing to when and how to use them, prepare to dive deeper into the complex yet fascinating domain of database optimization.

Let's embark on this journey to leverage potent database techniques, particularly SQL Indexing, and lay a robust foundation for smart, strategic data management.

Chapter 3. Basics of Database Indexing

Before delving into the practical application of SQL indexing techniques, it's important to first understand the fundamentals of this concept. Database indexing is a technique that optimizes data retrieval operations, making the process substantially faster than conducting full-table scans to find related data.

3.1. What is an Index?

In the context of databases, an index is a data structure that facilitates speedy data retrieval operations on a database table at the cost of additional memory and writes. It is similar to an index at the end of a book that contains a list of keywords along with the pages where these keywords can be found.

Every database index holds a set of pointers to the rows in a table, sorted by a certain 'indexed' field. Indexing therefore allows quicker access to rows associated with the field's values, even if those rows are widely scattered throughout the table.

3.2. Types of Indexes

There are several types of database indexes, each having its distinct use and function. Some of the main types include:

- B-tree Index: The most common type of index that many databases implement by default. B-tree indexes can handle equality and range queries on data that can be sorted into some order.

- Hash Index: Best used for equality comparisons and can provide constant-time performance for these operations. However, hash indexes aren't efficient in finding the next entry in a sequence, so range queries or sorting aren't well supported.

- Bitmap Index: It uses bit arrays (commonly called bitmaps) and answers queries by performing bitwise logical operations on these bitmaps. They are best used in situations where the number of distinct indexed values is low compared to the number of rows in the table.

- Clustered Index: In this, the order of the rows in the database corresponds to the order of the index, reducing the reading time for large chunks of data.

- Non-Clustered Index: Here, the order of the rows doesn't correspond to the order of the index. Hence, they might need to perform more reads per query but can maintain multiple indexes per table.

3.3. How Indexing Works?

When you create an index on a database, it sorts the values from the indexed columns and pairs them with a reference to where the related data can be found. The process is akin to the way a book index sorts keywords alphabetically with page references.

Indexes can significantly improve query performance, but they do come with their own costs. It begins with storage - indexes need disk space. Also, while read operations can become faster due to the presence of indexes, write operations (like INSERT, UPDATE, DELETE) can become slower as indexes need to be updated as well when these operations are performed.

3.4. When to Use Indexing?

Determining when to use database indexing requires an understanding of the nature of the queries that would run on the database and the type of data it would contain.

If a table is frequently written to but seldom read, the costs of maintaining the index might outweigh the benefits. But when a table is frequently subjected to read operations, or when table scans are slow due to the large volume of data, indexing can drastically improve performance.

For columns that have a wide range of unique value, like an ID or timestamp, indexing can expedite lookup and range queries. Columns that tend to have many null values or have boolean data can also benefit from indexing.

3.5. Steps to Create Index

Creating an index typically involves issuing a command such as `CREATE INDEX`. Here's an example in SQL:

```
CREATE INDEX index_name
ON table_name (column_name);
```

In this statement, `index_name` is the name of the index, `table_name` is the name of the table to be indexed, and `column_name` is the name of the column on which the index is to be created.

Despite its apparent simplicity, indexing requires a solid understanding of its principles and appropriate usage to avoid inefficiencies and to leverage its benefits optimally. Through mastering these basics, one can proficiently navigate database indexing, enhancing the speed and efficiency of database-related operations.

Chapter 4. Exploring SQL Indexing: A Deep Dive

Databases are the lifeblood of any application, managing the flow of information that propels our digital society. Central to any database is its query performance, and in SQL (Structured Query Language)-based databases, a foundational technique for optimizing this performance is indexing.

But what is an SQL index? Why is it so significant, and how can we leverage it for maximum database efficiency? In this comprehensive dive into SQL indexing, we will answer these questions and more, providing an in-depth exploration into this important technology.

4.1. What is an SQL Index?

An SQL index is a data structure that improves the speed of operations in a database table. Much like the index in a book, which lets you quickly find specific information without scanning each page, an SQL index provides swift access to desired data without searching every row in a database table.

Indexes are created using a few columns in a table. When you create an index on a column or set of columns, you're essentially creating a data structure (like a B-tree or hash) which holds a sorted list of the records based on these columns. This ordered list allows SQL Server to find the data pointed to by the index incredibly quickly.

4.2. SQL Index Types

You'll come across several types of indexes in SQL, and understanding their uses and characteristics is crucial for effective database optimization. Here are a few to keep in mind:

4.2.1. Clustered Indexes

A clustered index determines the physical order of data in a table. Therefore, a table can have only one clustered index. If clustered indexes are properly used, they can increase database performance by reducing the disk IO operations.

4.2.2. Non-Clustered Indexes

Unlike a clustered index, a non-clustered index doesn't sort the physical data inside the table. Instead, it maintains a separate record of data each containing the non-clustered index key and a pointer to the record having the key. A table can have multiple non-clustered indexes.

4.2.3. Unique Indexes

A unique index does not allow for any duplicate values to be inserted into the table. The uniqueness property of an index ensures that the index key contains no duplicate entries for any column.

4.2.4. Bitmap Indexes

Bitmap indexes are used in situations where there are a limited number of distinct values. These indexes map each distinct column-value to a list of rows that possess that value, which can greatly speed up certain types of queries.

4.2.5. Full-Text Indexes

Full-text indexes in SQL Server lets users and applications run full-text queries against character-based data in SQL Server tables.

Once the syntax and characteristics of index types have been understood, we can then move towards the methods of creating and using indices.

4.3. Creating and Using SQL Indexes

Creating indexes in SQL depends on the specific database management system (DBMS) you are using. However, in most cases, the CREATE INDEX statement is utilized.

For instance, to create an index on a "Customers" table, within which the "LastName" is the column to be indexed, you might use a command such as:

```
CREATE INDEX idx_lastname
ON Customers (LastName);
```

When using the SELECT statement to query the database, the SQL server determines whether to use an index based on the tables, joins, and criteria used in the query. If it is more efficient to scan the entire table due to the nature of the query, it will choose not to use the index.

4.4. Improving Performance with SQL Indexes

Proper use of SQL indexing can give massive performance boosts. If your application involves complex queries consuming a significant amount of resources, you'll likely see a drastic improvement in query performance when appropriate indexes are used.

Indexes reduce the number of disk accesses required when a query is executed. For instance, if a query with a WHERE clause is run without an index, the SQL server must scan the entire table to find the relevant row(s). This operation, known as a 'table scan', can be slow and resource-intensive for large databases. But with an index, the SQL server can find relevant rows quickly, without scanning the entire table.

However, while indexing can optimize reading from a database, it can have the opposite effect on write operations (INSERT, UPDATE, DELETE). This is due to the overhead of maintaining the index data structure.

Hence, finding an optimal balance of indexed over unindexed data and read over write operations is crucial to getting real performance benefits out of indexes.

4.5. Best Practices for SQL Indexing

Knowing how to index is essential, but knowing when and where to use indexing makes all the difference. Here are a few best practices to guide your indexing strategy:

- Don't index every column: While indexes improve read efficiency, they degrade write efficiency. Indexing every column in a database will drastically slow down the speed at which you can write/modify data.

- Carefully consider your queries: Index the columns that you frequently query. These columns are typically those included in WHERE, ORDER BY, GROUP BY, JOIN clauses.

- Keep your indexes as narrow as possible: This reduces the size of your index and reduces the number of disk I/O reads.

- Make sure your indexes are selective: Highly selective indexes, those where the indexed column contains a high number of unique values, are more efficient.

- Regularly maintain and rebuild your indexes: Over time, as data changes, your indexes will become fragmented leading to decreased performance. Regular database maintenance should include tasks to rebuild or reorganize indexes.

In conclusion, SQL indexing is an exceptional tool for database optimization. It's not only a technical skill, but a strategic one that can have a significant impact on the performance and efficiency of a system. Understanding indexing inside and out thus equips you with a quintessential skill required in the world of effective data management.

Chapter 5. The Core Principles of Efficient Indexing

Establishing efficient indexing in a database gives it wings. The general idea revolves around creating "shortcuts" to data in order to speed up retrieval times. A well-structured index utilizes considerably less disk space and can retrieve data much faster compared to solely searching through every record in the database. However, building an efficient index that facilitates quick reads and doesn't unduly burden write operations necessitates understanding crucial principles. In this section, we explore four core principles that will help you design and maintain efficient indexes.

5.1. The Principle of Selectivity

Selectivity is a concept central to effective indexing. It is determined by the number of unique values in a certain field, relative to the total number of records. Highly selective indexes have a large proportion of unique values, and it's these indexes that usually provide the most performance benefits.

Consider a table of customers consisting of many fields such as customer ID, name, age, gender, etc. An index on the 'customer ID' field, which is unique for each customer, would be significantly more selective than an index on the 'gender' field, which mostly likely has only a few distinct values (male, female). Consequently, it takes less time to locate information using a selective index, thus making them more efficient.

Here is an understanding of why selectivity is important. Consider the following table:

Index	Number of Unique Entries	Total Entries
Customer ID	1000000	1000000
Gender	2	1000000

As you can see, the 'Customer ID' index is much more selective than the 'Gender' index. Thus, if you're trying to find one specific customer, it's much faster to search the Customer ID index than the Gender index.

5.2. The Principle of Proper Ordering

The second principle revolves around proper ordering. Indexes can be constructed on multiple columns in a table, called a composite index. Attention to the order of columns when creating such indexes is crucial to optimize their efficiency.

Consider a table with fields such as 'City', 'Street', and 'House Number'. Suppose a majority of your queries involve searching by 'City' and 'Street'. In such a scenario, the order of columns in the index should be 'City', 'Street', and then 'House Number'. If the order placed 'City' after 'Street', the index would not be efficient for city-wise searches.

This principle is best understood through a real-world analogy. Suppose you're looking for a book in a library. The books are arranged first by subject (City), within which they are organized by author's name (Street), and then by the year of publication (House Number). If you were to find a specific book knowing its subject and author's name, you naturally wouldn't start your search with the year of publication — instead, you'd navigate first through the subject and then the author before reaching the relevant publication year.

5.3. The Principle of Right-Sized Indexing

Thirdly, the principle of right-sized indexing emerges as an important consideration. It reflects knowing when not to index. Indexing accelerates data retrieval but at the cost of additional storage and slower write operations.

Every time data is inserted, updated, or deleted from the table, all associated indexes must be updated as well. Therefore, having too many indexes or indexing unnecessary columns can lead to performance degradation, contradicting the overall aim of indexing. This involves careful analysis of your query patterns and deciding which columns ought to be indexed keeping in context the balance between read and write operations.

One needs to deliberate over the type of queries commonly used. If a particular column is rarely part of a WHERE clause or JOIN condition, it's less likely to be a suitable candidate for indexing. On the other hand, columns that frequently appear in such expressions are prime candidates for the indexing boost.

5.4. The Principle of Index Maintenance

The fourth principle encourages regular index maintenance. Over time, as data is added, changed, and removed, the database index can become fragmented. This fragmentation can degrade the performance of the index, turning it essentially ineffective.

Regular index maintenance, involving operations such as rebuilding or reorganizing the indexes, helps keep it efficient. These operations regroup information, eliminate unused space, and update statistics about the index that the database uses to build optimal query plans.

Index maintenance should be performed regularly, and, if possible, during off-peak hours, as these operations can be resource-intensive and might affect system performance during execution.

To summarize, efficient indexing involves a deep understanding of the data at hand and how it's utilized. The success of the techniques relies on the principles of selectivity, proper ordering, right-sized indexing, and regular maintenance. By correctly implementing these principles, you can achieve a responsive and performant database system capable of supporting quick data retrieval with minimal lag. This, in turn, empowers your database users, whether they are business analysts, software applications, or end-users, with the ability to access the data they need quickly and accurately.

Chapter 6. Analyzing Data Access Patterns

Analyzing data access patterns is an intrinsic aspect of optimizing your database performance using SQL indexing. Understanding the data requests your database receives can guide you in creating indexes that enhance speed and efficiency.

6.1. Uncovering the Basics

Every time you interact with your database—either by running an SQL query to fetch data or performing an insert, update, or delete action—an access pattern is created. This pattern portrays how your application or service uses the database, thereby providing profound insights into the most frequent queries, accessed fields, read-to-write ratios, and more. By studying these patterns, you can make informed decisions on where to establish indexes, and the type of indexes suitable for your data needs.

6.2. Query Frequency and Hotspots

Plunging into the specifics, the first step to evaluate the data access patterns is to examine the frequency of the various SQL queries. By identifying the most used queries, the 'hotspots', you can pinpoint where to establish or improve indexing.

A query log, an essential feature in almost all database management systems, can be an excellent place to start. It will record all the different queries run against your database. Additionally, you might consider enabling slow query logs to identify those long-running queries, taking over a certain threshold of execution time. Tools like MySQL's 'EXPLAIN' command, or similar in other databases, can aid in understanding the query execution plan and recognizing the areas where indexing can help.

6.3. Read-to-Write Ratio

Another important facet to examine is the ratio of read operations to write operations. In scenarios where the database reads far outweigh the writes, adding more indexes can be beneficial as they can make read queries faster. On the contrary, if your application performs more writes (inserts, updates, deletes), limit your indexing. Every index you add also needs to be updated during a write operation, slowing down the system performance.

6.4. Identifying Accessed Fields

Further, understanding which fields are accessed the most by your queries can guide you on where to establish indexes. By indexing these frequently accessed fields, you can notably speed up data retrieval. Keep in mind, however, the data type of the field and its cardinality should be considered as certain indexes work better with specific data types and high cardinality fields.

6.5. Considering Data Sorting

Queries often involve sorting data in a specific order. In such cases, consider indexes that maintain data in a specific order, such as B-tree indexes. They allow for faster retrieval of sorted data and range searches, thereby enhancing query performance.

6.6. Order of Columns in Multi-Column Indexes

When creating multiple-column indexes, the order of columns is crucial. To decide the optimal order, evaluate how your queries are using these columns. SQL Server, for instance, can use a multi-column index for a query that involves only the first column listed in it. However, if a query involves the second column but not the first, the index cannot provide any benefit.

6.7. Designing for the Future

Through this process, it's imperative to remember that data access patterns change over time, especially as more data accumulates and business requirements shift. What works now may not work in the future. Regularly reviewing and updating access patterns analysis can go a long way in ensuring that your systems remain optimal and efficient.

Analyzing data access patterns is about embracing a proactive, data-driven mindset. By regularly evaluating how your applications interact with your database, you can stay ahead of performance issues and ensure that your systems remain fast, efficient, and reliable. With a solid understanding of data access patterns and effective indexing, you can ensure your database remains robust and performant, catering to your evolving business needs with grace and speed.

Remember: an optimized database isn't just about speed—it's about creating a foundation for scalable, sustainable growth.

Chapter 7. Balancing Indexes for Optimal Performance

The management and maintenance of indexes is of paramount importance in database management. Notary is this true than when it comes to performance optimization, where indexes play an instrumental role in expediting the querying process. However, simply having indexes on your database isn't sufficient. You need to strike an equilibrium among indexes to ensure optimal performance. This chapter will elucidate the intricacies of balancing indexes and how it helps optimize the overall database performance.

=== Understanding Indexing Balance

By index balancing, we refer to the strategic creation and management of indexes in a database to not only minimize data retrieval time but also to ensure there's minimal overhead while writing data into the database. It is the delicate middle-ground which warrants proficient execution of both 'Read' and 'Write' operations. Unregulated indexing can lead to a phenomenon known as Over-indexing, which becomes a bane for write operations, causing the database performance to sag.

7.1. Over-indexing and Its Pitfalls

Over-indexing occurs when too many indexes are created on the database. While this might seem like a good idea to accelerate read operations, it can dramatically slow down write operations like INSERT, UPDATE, and DELETE. Each time a data row is inserted or amended, associated indexes must also be updated. If there are too many indexes, the overhead for writes increases substantially.

Maintaining excess indexes isn't just detrimental to writing speed, it also demands more storage space, resulting in inefficient use of resources.

=== Strategies for Balancing Indexes

Different strategies can be employed to achieve a balance in indexing. Their choice and application will depend on various factors like the nature of your application, the mix of read and write operations, and even the resources at your disposal.

1. Analyzing Your Workload: The first step to balancing indexes is to understand the workload. Identify whether your system is read-heavy or write-heavy. For example, if your system is largely read-heavy, it might make sense to have more indexes, as read performance is pivotal.

2. Selective Indexing: Index only the most frequently used columns. Monitoring query performance over a time can help you zero in on which columns are being used most often in WHERE clauses.

3. Using the Right Index Types: Different DBMS offer various types of indexes such as B-trees, Bitmaps, Clustered, and Non-clustered indexes. Their application hinges on the nature of data and the types of queries executed.

4. Index Partitioning: This involves segmenting an index into smaller, more manageable pieces. It is useful in cases of large tables and can boost performance substantially.

7.2. Analyzing Index Usage

The above strategies will fall short if you don't have an understanding of how your current indexes are performing. Many DBMS provide inbuilt statistics that can be queried to see how often indexes are being used.

For SQL Server, the sys.dm_db_index_usage_stats DMV can be used. With PostgreSQL, the pg_stat_user_indexes view can provide useful information about index usage. In Oracle, similar insights can be gathered using the Index Monitoring feature. You can use these tools to your advantage to periodically analyze and tune your indexes.

=== Rebuilding and Reorganizing Indexes

As data accumulates and changes over time, indexes can become fragmented, causing performance degradation. It's important to periodically rebuild or reorganize indexes.

- Rebuilding: Involves recreating the index. Use this option when the index is highly fragmented.

- Reorganizing: This process physically reorders the leaf-level pages to match the B-tree logical order (left to right). This is a less intrusive operation and can be done when the index has relatively lower fragmentation.

Auto maintenance tasks can be scheduled in SQL Server using the SQL Server Agent, which can conduct a weekly or monthly maintenance regimen depending on database usage.

7.3. Conclusion

Database performance optimization and particularly, balancing indexes, may seem like a daunting task. However, with a keen understanding of your workload, thoughtful selection and use of indexes, regular monitoring and maintenance, striking the right balance becomes inevitable. This delicate equilibrium is a crucial step towards ensuring your database remains responsive and resilient under diverse usage loads, a goal that is within your sight now. Seek to apply what you've learned from this chapter and embark on the quest to make the most efficient use of your data. Remember, the process is iterative and you're bound to see improvements as you keep refining your indexing strategy.

Chapter 8. Overcoming Common Indexing Pitfalls

Indexing may seem like a magic bullet for database optimization, but like most powerful tools, it needs to be used judiciously to avoid potential pitfalls. A deep understanding of how SQL indexes work is key to preventing and troubleshooting common blunders. In this chapter, we will equip you with the knowledge you need to confidently handle index issues.

8.1. The Costs of Over-Indexing

Perhaps the most common pitfall associated with SQL indexing is over-indexing. To a novice, it might make sense to apply an index to every column in every database table. After all, if indexes speed up queries, more is better, right? Wrong. Indexing comes with its own set of costs.

Indexes, while expediting queries, consume storage resources as they store a copy of the data along with the database. More indexes mean more storage overhead. Beyond that, each index you add increases the time it takes to write to the table. Every time a write operation (INSERT, UPDATE or DELETE) is performed, your database needs to update every index associated with the table. Thus, too many indexes can slow down write operations significantly.

To avoid over-indexing, it's crucial to understand and analyse the nature of your data and queries. Only index columns that are frequently used in WHERE, JOIN, ORDER BY, or GROUP BY clauses. Database profiling tools can be a great help in this process by analyzing query patterns and recommending optimal indexes.

8.2. Understanding Index Types

Another common pitfall involves misunderstanding the types of indexes and when to use each. Broadly speaking, there are two types of indexes: clustered and non-clustered. Each has its own strengths and weaknesses.

Clustered indexes determine the physical order of data in a table, making them highly efficient for range queries. However, you can only have one clustered index per table, hence knowledge of the most queried data range is crucial. Non-clustered indexes use a separate structure to hold data pointers, useful when a full data read is unnecessary.

Choosing a wrong index type for your specific use-case can have several downsides like increased storage usage, increased cache miss rate, and slower query performance. It's crucial to pick an index type that matches your data access patterns.

8.3. Dealing with Index Fragmentation

Over time, as you continually insert, update, and delete records in a table, your indexes will fragment. This fragmentation results in slower query times and inefficient use of storage. While modern databases often handle minor fragmentation with little impact on performance, extreme cases require intervention.

To spot index fragmentation, use built-in database functions or third-party tools that report fragmentation percentage. If the level of fragmentation is high, consider reorganizing or rebuilding the index. Reorganizing is less resource intensive and can be done while the database is online, but rebuilding often results in a more compact and efficient index.

8.4. Handling Null Values in Indexes

Finally, let's talk about null values in indexes. Databases handle null properties in different ways. In some cases, these null values can slow down your queries, or worse, can lead you to the wrong results.

If nullable columns are often included in your queries, you might want to consider using a partial index that only includes rows where your column is not null. Alternatively, you may decide to implement a known value when data does not exist to avoid having null values at all.

Understanding and correcting these pitfalls is critical for optimizing database performance. As you have learned, over-indexing, misunderstanding index types, ignoring index fragmentation, and mishandling null values are challenges, but by equipping yourself with the knowledge to handle them, you can ensure a resilient and responsive database system. Through careful planning, regular monitoring, and maintenance, databases can be optimized using SQL indexing techniques to ensure speedy data retrieval and efficient system performance.

The effective use of data is pivotal to business strategy, operations, and success. Therefore, mastering these techniques and avoiding common pitfalls will level up your database management skills and strategies. This arsenal of knowledge will help you meet the challenges of an increasingly data-driven world head on.

Chapter 9. Practical Examples: Implementing SQL Indexing Techniques

Query optimization and performance improvement can be achieved by using various SQL Indexing techniques. But the real understanding comes when we see these concepts at work, in practical scenarios. In this chapter, we'll be walking through a number of examples, implementing and learning from each SQL indexing technique involved.

9.1. Introduction to SQL Indexes

An SQL index is a database object that improves the speed of data retrieval operations. It works in the same way as an index in a book by referring to the pages wherein information lies, instead of searching all the pages. Hence, using indexes can speed up data retrieval.

Just as you don't really read through every single page when you are looking for a particular topic in a book, SQL Server doesn't scan every row in a table. This is where an index comes in—essentially, it tells the SQL Server where that data row is.

9.2. Creating an Index

A simple command to create an index is illustrated below:

```
CREATE INDEX index_name
ON table_name (column1, column2, ...);
```

This command is generally used to create indexes in most of the SQL databases. Here, we see a basic index on Column1 and Column2 of the Table_Name.

Here, `index_name` is the name of the index, and `table_name` is the name of the table to be indexed. Columns `column1`, `column2` ... represent the columns included in the index.

9.3. Single-Column Indexes

A single-column index is an index created on a single table column. Let's consider an example of an SQL database for a library, where books data is stored in the 'Library' Table.

```
CREATE INDEX library_index
ON Library (Book_Id);
```

In the Library table, 'Book_Id' can be a column where a user might frequently search for information. Hence, creating an index on these columns can speed up such searches.

9.4. Unique Indexes

A unique index ensures the data contained in the column or combination of two columns is unique in every respect. It helps prevent duplicate entries in the column.

To illustrate, let's use the 'User' Table of an application that has a 'User Id' and 'Email' fields. Both these columns must have unique data.

Here's how we can create a unique index:

```
CREATE UNIQUE INDEX user_profile_index
```

```
ON User (User_Id, Email);
```

9.5. Composite Indexes

Composite indexes, also known as multiple-column indexes, are defined on more than one column of a table which offers a way to enhance database performance.

Considering a 'Sales' table that contains 'Year', 'Month', and 'Day' as the columns. Let's say a common query is to find sales between two particular dates.

To speed up this search, a composite index could be set on the 'Year', 'Month', and 'Day' columns.

```
CREATE INDEX date_Sales_Index
ON Sales (Year, Month, Day);
```

9.6. Using Indexes in Queries

Indexes can be implemented within SQL queries. When writing a SQL query, order your conditions to take maximum advantage of the indexes. If an index exists on the columns being used in the WHERE clause, retrieval will be much faster.

Considering a 'Sales' table with an index on the 'Year', 'Month', and 'Day' columns, you may write:

```
SELECT *
FROM Sales
WHERE Year = 2020 AND Month = 05 AND Day = 21;
```

The query will utilize the 'date_Sales_Index' for a faster data retrieval.

9.7. Explaining Queries with Indexes

By using the EXPLAIN keyword, we can get a breakdown of how a query was executed by an SQL server, including the use of indexes.

```
EXPLAIN SELECT *
FROM Sales
WHERE Year = 2020 AND Month = 05 AND Day = 21;
```

This would help in understanding how the index was used and how the decision was made by the database to use that index.

9.8. Conclusion

While the above examples provide a brief overview of SQL Indexing Techniques, remember that the key to efficient use of indexes lies in understanding the specific requirements of your database, how queries are processed, and what kind of data retrieval patterns are more frequent. While indexes can greatly improve data retrieval speed, inappropriate or excessive use of indexing may result in reduction of overall database performance due to overheads associated with updating and maintaining indexes. Use them judiciously, and they can be your best aid in optimizing SQL database performance.

In the upcoming chapters, we'll discuss more advanced indexing concepts and their implementations, fine-tuning your understanding of database optimization.

Chapter 10. Advanced SQL Indexing Strategies

The pursuit of the ideal SQL indexing strategy begins with a solid understanding of the fundamental principles and factors that influence index performance. Before delving into specific techniques, it's essential to grasp the potential impacts of indexing on transaction processing, query time, disk space usage, and maintenance needs.

10.1. Understanding Index Types

Before we discuss advanced strategies, we need a broad understanding of index types available in SQL.

```
* Clustered Index: This type determines the physical
order of data in a table and each table can have only
one clustered index.
* Non-clustered Index: Differing from the clustered
index, a table can have multiple non-clustered indexes.
It does not sort the physical data inside the table,
instead, it uses a logical order.
* Unique Index: The unique index does not allow the
field to have duplicate values if the column is unique
indexed. It can be clustered or non-clustered.
* Filtered Index: A filtered index is used to index a
portion of rows in a table, which improves query
performance, reduces index maintenance costs, and
reduces index storage costs.
```

An efficient indexing strategy relies on the judicious use of these types based on data characteristics and the nature of queries the database has to serve.

10.2. Query Analysis for Index Optimization

A proper indexing strategy involves an informed study of the queries that the database regularly deals with. Some pointers include:

- Identify frequently run operations. These typically include SELECT, UPDATE, and DELETE statements.

- Analyze 'WHERE', 'ORDER BY' and 'JOIN' clauses since these are often involved in retrieval or modification operations.

- PAY attention to grouping and aggregation functions used in queries.

- Inspect your database's query execution plans, which provide information on how a SQL server will execute a query.

Based on these observations, index fields that are often involved in filtering, sorting, or joining operations.

10.3. Index Selection and Placement

When it comes to choosing the right index, consider the aspects like:

- Cardinality: Fields with high cardinality, i.e., a high number of unique values, are excellent choices for indexing.

- Frequency of Updates: Indexes speed up data retrieval but slow down data modification. Therefore, consider how frequently a column used in an index is updated.

When deciding on which drive to store your index, remember that indexes and data files frequently read together should be stored separately. This is because reading from two different drives is faster than one.

10.4. Column Order in Composite Indexes

The order of columns in composite indexes has a significant impact on its efficiency. As a rule of thumb, the column used in the WHERE clause filter condition more often should come first. However, other factors such as column cardinality and selectivity may also influence the order of columns.

10.5. Covering Index

A covering index, which includes all the columns referenced by a query, can greatly improve performance as the database server can find all the needed data within the index itself without looking up the main table.

10.6. Making use of Indexed Views

Indexed views can be a great alternative for frequently joined tables with complex queries. This allows you to store the result set of a query involving joins and aggregations physically and update it whenever the underlying data changes.

10.7. Dealing with Index Fragmentation

Index fragmentation can lead to decreased performance. Regular monitoring of fragmentation levels, with periodic defragmentation, can help to maintain optimal performance. SQL Server provides 'Rebuild' and 'Reorganize' options to deal with fragmentation.

10.8. Consider Partitioning

Partitioning enables segmenting a single large table into smaller, more manageable parts - almost like creating smaller tables within a large table. It can significantly enhance query performance, particularly on large tables.

Remember, indexing is more than creating indexes for each table. It involves a in-depth understanding of your data, your usage patterns, and continuous refinement based on performance analysis. Benefits of a well thought indexing strategy can be manifold - faster data retrieval, efficient use of storage, and more responsive application performance.

Chapter 11. Future Trends in Database Indexing

As indexing technologies continue to evolve, it's become evident that the future of database indexing will be shaped by three significant trends: automation, platform flexibility, and advancement of distributed databases.

11.1. Automation in Database Indexing

With progressing technological advancements, there are increased efforts to make the task of index management more automated. This aspect could revolutionize database indexing in the future.

Traditionally, database administrators (DBAs) have had the responsibility to maintain indexes. This includes decisions about which indexes to create, based on the query workload. Unfortunately, this process is not error-free. A lack of knowledge or oversight could lead to selection of inappropriate indexes, leading to underperforming systems.

However, with the advent of machine learning and artificial intelligence, there is a significant shift towards automation in indexing. This trend involves AutoIndexing or Automatic Index Tuning, where machine learning algorithms are used to analyze the workload and automating the process of creating, updating, and deleting indexes.

This transition to automation hails several benefits. It not only frees up DBAs from frequent tuning actions, thereby enabling them to focus on more strategic tasks, but also helps in performing index management more accurately and efficiently, which leads to significantly improved application performance.

11.2. Platform Flexibility

Platform flexibility, or the ability for an indexing mechanism to function seamlessly across various database systems, is another significant trend.

In the past, indexing strategies were often tightly coupled to specific database management systems. As a result, an indexing strategy working well for one system might not work efficiently for another. This lack of uniformity caused significant bottlenecks, especially for organizations working with multiple database systems.

Moving forward, there is a clear trend towards the development of more flexible indexing strategies. These strategies are compatible across different types of database systems- be it relational or NoSQL databases. This ensures effective and efficient functioning, irrespective of the underlying database management system.

Moreover, the rise of cloud-based database services like Amazon RDS, Google Cloud SQL, and Microsoft Azure SQL Database is further strengthening the need for platform flexibility. For these services, it's important to have an indexing system that can function efficiently across different cloud platforms.

11.3. Advancement of Distributed Databases

The emergence and advancement of distributed databases is another trend that is shaping the future of database indexing.

Distributed databases are databases in which storage devices are not all attached to a common processor but are dispersed throughout a network. Such databases support impressive scalability and can handle huge volumes of data across a distributed network of storage.

However, the unique nature and structure of distributed databases vault new challenges in indexing. Traditional indexing techniques, which work well on a single, unified database, struggle with effective execution on a distributed database. This is because these techniques don't take into account data distribution across different nodes or the network's latency.

To overcome these challenges, new indexing techniques are being developed. Techniques such as distributed hash indexes and bitmap indexes are promising solutions that can improve the performance of distributed databases significantly.

In conclusion, the future of database indexing is marked by advancements in automation, platform flexibility, and progression of distributed databases. As technology continues to evolve, these trends will further define the scope and functioning of database indexing. More than ever before, practitioners and leaders engaged in data management need to stay abreast of these trends to align their strategies with the future and optimize their database systems effectively.

To stay updated with these trends, keep researching, learning, and experimenting. The future is not something we enter—it is something we create.

By being aware of these trends, understanding their implications, and adapting to these changes, we can ensure that our database systems are not just robust and resilient, but also future-ready. As we step into the future, these trends will be instrumental in guiding our path, shaping our strategies, and ensuring our success in the world of database systems.

www.ingramcontent.com/pod-product-compliance
Lightning Source LLC
LaVergne TN
LVHW051634050326
832903LV00033B/4748